All about TRUCKS

CHEVROLET TRUCKS

By Linda Hopkins

AV2
www.av2books.com

All about TRUCKS

CHEVROLET TRUCKS

CONTENTS

2 AV2 Book Code
4 Chevrolet Trucks
6 Louis Chevrolet
8 The Logo
10 Chevrolet through History
12 Chevrolet Silverado 1500
14 “Find New Roads”
16 How It’s Made
18 Today’s Lineup
20 Tomorrow’s Chevrolet
22 Chevrolet Quiz
23 Key Words/Index

California
PTS

CHEVROLET TRUCKS

Ever since the first factory-built pickup trucks were made, pickups have been used to transport heavy loads. At the front of a pickup truck is the **cab**, where the driver and passengers sit. The open area at the back of the truck is called the **cargo** area. It has low sides and a **tailgate** at the back.

Chevrolet, a motor car company, was bought by General Motors in 1918. That same year, Chevrolet sold its first truck. In 1960, Chevrolet introduced the C10. The C10 was the forerunner of the Silverado, which is Chevrolet's most popular modern model. Today, Chevrolet pickups are among the best-selling trucks in North America.

About **1.8 million** Chevrolet vehicles were sold in **2020.**

The **2006 Silverado Intimidator SS** is **one of the rarest** Chevrolet vehicles.

Only **933 units** of the **2006 Silverado Intimidator SS** were ever made.

LOUIS CHEVROLET

"Movement is the universal language of personal freedom."
-Louis Chevrolet

Louis Chevrolet was an automotive designer and a race car driver. He was born on Christmas Day, 1878, in Neuchâtel, Switzerland. In 1900, he moved to the United States, where he joined the Fiat auto racing team. Along with **entrepreneur** William Durant, he started the Chevrolet Motor Company in 1911.

Durant and Chevrolet soon realized that their dreams for the new company were not the same. Chevrolet sold his **shares** to Durant. However, the company kept Chevrolet's name.

As a race car driver, Louis Chevrolet was recognized for his daring on the racetrack.

MAPPING CHEVROLET TODAY

Chevrolet's main headquarters are in Detroit, Michigan, where the first Chevrolet vehicles were made.

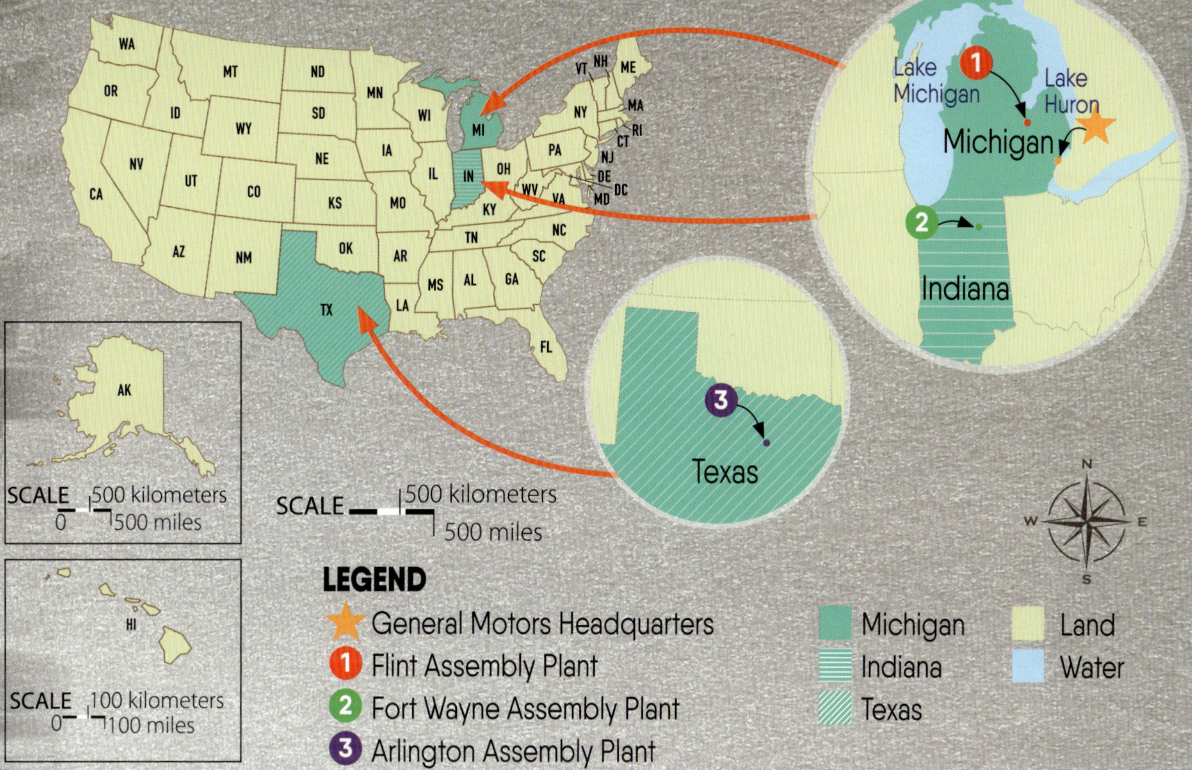

1 *Flint Assembly Plant* Flint, Michigan

Current products: Chevrolet Silverado
Year opened: 1947
Site size: 159 acres (64 hectares)
People employed: 5,434

2 *Fort Wayne Assembly Plant* Roanoke, Indiana

Current products: Chevrolet Silverado 1500
Year opened: 1986
Site size: 716 acres (290 ha)
People employed: 4,424

3 *Arlington Assembly Plant* Arlington, Texas

Current products: Chevrolet Tahoe, Chevrolet Suburban
Year opened: 1954
Site size: 250 acres (101 ha)
People employed: 5,677

THE LOGO

The famous bowtie shape of the Chevrolet logo was first introduced to the world in 1914. It appeared on a car called the Chevrolet H2 Royal Mail. Chevrolet's co-founder, William Durant, said that the idea for the shape came from the wallpaper design in a Paris hotel room. Since 1914, the logo's colors and fonts have changed, but its shape has remained the same.

Today, the Chevrolet logo is typically gold. However, in 2014, Chevrolet introduced the "flowtie" on some vehicles. The flowtie is different from other logos. It is hollow, which allows air to pass through.

CHEVROLET EMBLEM

Chevrolet introduced a redesigned bowtie with additional texture in 2011.

The gold color of Chevrolet's bowtie is meant to reflect power and confidence.

CHEVROLET THROUGH HISTORY

Americans have been driving Chevrolets since the early 20th century. To this day, Chevrolets remain popular throughout the United States.

1918

Chevrolet sells its first pickup truck, launching itself as a truck manufacturer.

1960

Chevrolet introduces the C10 pickup truck.

1975

A **trim** called the Silverado is offered on the C10.

1999

The Chevrolet Silverado is produced as a stand-alone model for the first time. It wins Motor Trend's Truck of the Year award.

2009

Chevrolet introduces a **hybrid** Silverado. It is discontinued in 2013.

2019

The fourth generation of Silverados is introduced.

CHEVROLET SILVERADO 1500

The Chevrolet Silverado 1500 is one of the best-selling trucks in North America. It was developed from the C/K line of trucks that Chevrolet introduced in 1960. The Silverado is a **versatile** truck. It is stylish, comfortable for traveling, and a powerful **workhorse**.

In 2020, the Chevrolet Silverado was the second most popular pickup truck in the United States.

The Chevrolet Silverado has more sales than any other vehicle sold by General Motors.

Country music artists often sing songs about their pickup trucks. In the last twenty years, there have been more songs about Chevrolet trucks than any other pickup. Chevrolet even has its own TikTok account, with the first posted video featuring hip-hop artist Breland singing "My Truck." Country singers Luke Bryan and Brad Paisley both drive Chevrolet Silverados, as does celebrity Kourtney Kardashian.

More than 19 million Chevrolet Silverados have been sold in the United States.

"FIND NEW ROADS"

Chevrolet's slogan, "Find New Roads," is all about doing things differently. It suggests that Chevrolets will help their drivers face challenges and seek out new paths. Silverados are designed to go off-road without much difficulty and to manage in all weather conditions. They also make towing and hauling easier.

Chevrolet trucks can be **customized** according to the needs of the buyer. Someone buying a Silverado can choose from different engine sizes. The bigger the engine, the more weight a truck can carry. Buyers can also choose longer or shorter cargo beds and different cab sizes.

The Chevrolet Silverado 2500 HD is one of the most powerful trucks available.

FIND NEW ROADS™

The 2020 Silverado HD **can tow 35,500 pounds** (16,000 kilograms).

The **"Find New Roads"** slogan has been used since 2013.

Chevrolet adopted the "Find New Roads" slogan to better appeal to international markets.

HOW IT'S MADE

Almost all Silverados are bought and sold in North America. In the United States, most Silverados are built at the Fort Wayne plant in Indiana and the Flint plant in Michigan. Silverados are also made at the Silao, Guanajuato, plant in Mexico.

Building a truck is very complicated. The process uses advanced technology. People and robots work together to assemble each truck. Robots put all the parts together, while people do quality checks.

The Chevrolet Silverado 1500's body is made from a combination of steel and aluminum.

The Fort Wayne Assembly Plant only produces full-size pickup trucks.

The **Silverado 1500** has the **largest cargo bed** of all pickup trucks.

In 2019, General Motors invested $150 million to increase truck production at the Flint Assembly Plant.

The **2020 Silverado trucks** come with **seven different engine options.**

General Motors assembles both GMC and Chevrolet trucks at the Flint Assembly Plant.

TODAY'S LINEUP

Chevrolet has been making pickup trucks for more than 100 years. The Silverado is consistently one of the top three trucks sold in the United States and Canada. In addition to the full-size Silverado, Chevrolet also produces a mid-size truck, the Colorado.

Here are some of the Chevrolet trucks on the road today.

Chevrolet Colorado

Engine: **3.6L V6**

Horsepower: **308**

Maximum Towing Capacity: **7,700 pounds** (3,500 kg)

Starting Price: **$25,200**

Chevrolet Silverado 1500

Engine: **2.7L Turbo**

Horsepower: **310**

Maximum Towing Capacity: **13,300 pounds** (6,000 kg)

Starting Price: **$29,300**

Chevrolet Silverado 2500 HD

Engine: **6.6L V8**

Horsepower: **401**

Maximum Towing Capacity:
18,510 pounds (8,400 kg)

Starting Price: **$35,300**

Chevrolet Silverado 3500 HD

Engine: **6.6L V8**

Horsepower: **401**

Maximum Towing Capacity:
36,000 pounds (16,300 kg)

Starting Price: **$36,500**

TOMORROW'S CHEVROLET

Chevrolet is committed to **sustainability**. The company plans to introduce a range of electric vehicles to its lineup in the coming years. Chevrolet is also applying sustainability to the way it builds vehicles. The Arlington plant, for example, is completely powered by wind energy.

Chevrolet will introduce **Super Cruise**, a hands-free driving system, in the **2022 Silverado 1500**.

Chevrolet plans to introduce an **electric pickup truck** as early as **2023**.

Chevrolet's **electric pickup truck** may be able to drive more than **400 miles** (640 kilometers) on a single charge.

CHEVROLET QUIZ

1 When did Chevrolet sell its first pickup truck?

2 What was the name of Louis Chevrolet's business partner?

3 How is Chevrolet's flowtie different from its other logos?

4 Where are Chevrolet's main headquarters?

5 How many Silverados have been sold in the United States?

6 When was the Chevrolet Silverado first produced as a stand-alone model?

7 Which company owns Chevrolet?

8 What materials are the Silverado 1500's body made of?

9 What is Chevrolet's slogan?

10 What type of energy is used to power Chevrolet's Arlington plant?

ANSWERS
1. 1918 **2.** William Durant **3.** It is hollow **4.** Detroit, Michigan **5.** More than 19 million **6.** 1999 **7.** General Motors **8.** Aluminum and steel **9.** "Find New Roads" **10.** Wind energy

KEY WORDS

cab: the front part of a truck where the driver sits

cargo: goods carried by a ship, aircraft, truck, or other large vehicle

customized: changed in order to meet the specific needs or requirements of a person

entrepreneur: a person who starts new companies

hybrid: a vehicle that can run on both gas and electricity

shares: the portion given or belonging to one of a group of people owning something together

sustainability: involving methods that do not completely use up or destroy natural resources

tailgate: a door at the back of a truck or car, hinged at the bottom so that it opens downwards

trim: optional features for greater power, styling, and comfort

versatile: able to do many different kinds of things

workhorse: a vehicle or machine that proves to be durable and dependable

INDEX

Arlington Assembly Plant 7, 20, 22

C10 5, 10
Chevrolet Colorado 18
Chevrolet H2 Royal Mail 8
Chevrolet, Louis 6, 22
Chevrolet Silverado 1500 7, 12, 16, 17, 18, 21, 22
Chevrolet Silverado 2500 HD 14, 19
Chevrolet Silverado 3500 HD 19
Chevrolet Silverado Intimidator SS 5

Durant, William 6, 8, 22

electric vehicles 20, 21
engine 14, 17, 18, 19

"Find New Roads" 14, 15, 22
Flint Assembly Plant 7, 16, 17
Fort Wayne Assembly Plant 7, 16, 17

General Motors 5, 7, 13, 17, 22

logo 8, 9

Mexico 16

Super Cruise 21
Switzerland 6

United States 6, 10, 12, 13, 16, 18

Published by AV2
276 5th Avenue, Suite 704 #917
New York, NY 10001
Website: www.av2books.com

Library of Congress Cataloging-in-Publication Data

Names: Hopkins, Linda, author.
Title: Chevrolet trucks / Linda Hopkins.
Description: New York : AV2, [2022] | Series: All about trucks | Includes index. | Audience: Ages 8-12 | Audience: Grades 2-3
Identifiers: LCCN 2021023303 (print) | LCCN 2021023304 (ebook) | ISBN 9781791141844 (library binding) | ISBN 9781791141851 (paperback) | ISBN 9781791141868
Subjects: LCSH: Chevrolet trucks--Juvenile literature.
Classification: LCC TL230.5.C45 H66 2022 (print) | LCC TL230.5.C45 (ebook) | DDC 629.28/73--dc23
LC record available at https://lccn.loc.gov/2021023303
LC ebook record available at https://lccn.loc.gov/2021023304

Printed in Guangzhou, China
1 2 3 4 5 6 7 8 9 0 25 24 23 22 21

072021
101120

Art Director: Terry Paulhus **Project Coordinator:** Priyanka Das

Every reasonable effort has been made to trace ownership and to obtain permission to reprint copyright material. The publisher would be pleased to have any errors or omissions brought to its attention so that they may be corrected in subsequent printings.

The publisher acknowledges Alamy, Getty Images, Shutterstock, and Wikimedia as its primary image suppliers for this title.